WHOEVER YOU ARE

WHOEVER YOU ARE

By MEM FOX   Illustrated by LESLIE STAUB

Voyager Books
Harcourt, Inc.
San Diego   New York   London

www.harcourt.com

First Voyager Books edition 2001
Voyager Books is a trademark of Harcourt, Inc.,
registered in the United States of America and/or other jurisdictions.

The Library of Congress has cataloged the hardcover edition as follows:
Fox, Mem, 1946–
Whoever you are/Mem Fox; illustrated by Leslie Staub.
p. cm.
Summary: Despite the differences between people around the world,
there are similarities that join us together, such as pain, joy, and love.
1. Ethnicity—Juvenile literature.   2. Multiculturalism—Juvenile literature.
3. Individual differences—Juvenile literature.
[1. Ethnicity.   2. Multiculturalism.   3. Individuality.]
I. Staub, Leslie, 1957– ill. II. Title.
GN495.6.F69 1997
305.8—dc20   95-17887
ISBN 0-15-200787-3
ISBN 0-15-216406-5 pb

C E G H F D B

The illustrations in this book were done in oil on gessoed paper.
The hand-carved frames were made from plaster, wood, and faux gems.
The display type was hand lettered by Judythe Sieck.
The text type was set in Monotype Goudy Bold.
Color separations by Bright Arts Graphics Pte. Ltd., Singapore
Printed and bound by Tien Wah Press, Singapore
This book was printed on Arctic matte paper.
Production supervision by Sandra Grebenar and Wendi Taylor
Designed by Judythe Sieck

For Hanan Ashrawi
—M. F.

For YaYa
and for you,
whoever you are
—L. S.

Little one,
whoever you are,

wherever you are,

there are little ones
just like you
all over the world.

Their skin may be
different from yours,
and their homes may be
different from yours.

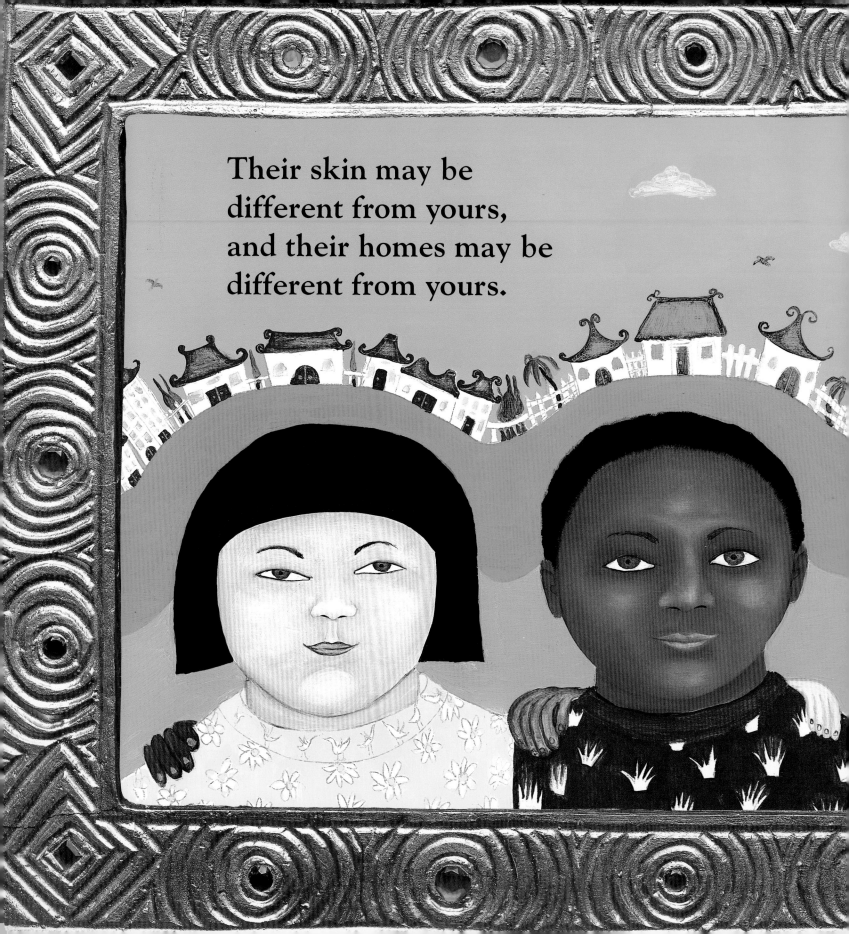

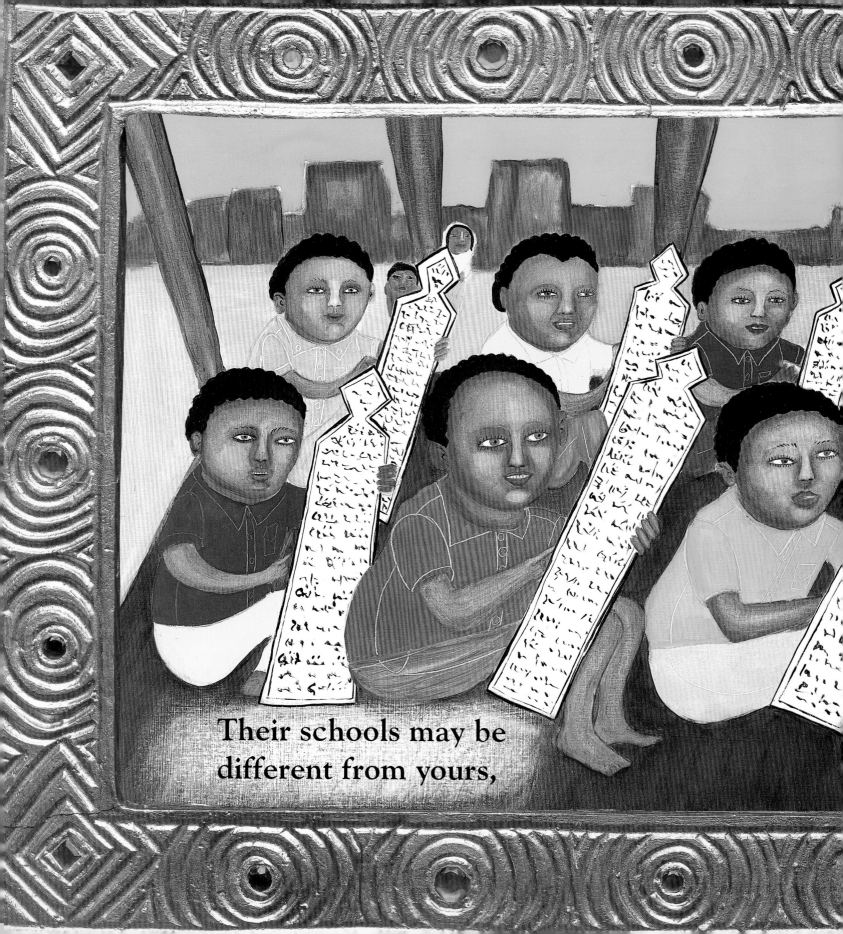

Their schools may be
different from yours,

and their lands may be
different from yours.

Their lives may be
different from yours,

and their words may be *very* different from yours.

whoever they are,
wherever they are,
all over the world.

Their smiles are like yours,

and they laugh just like you.

whoever they are,
wherever they are,
all over the world.

Little one,
when you are older
and when you are grown,

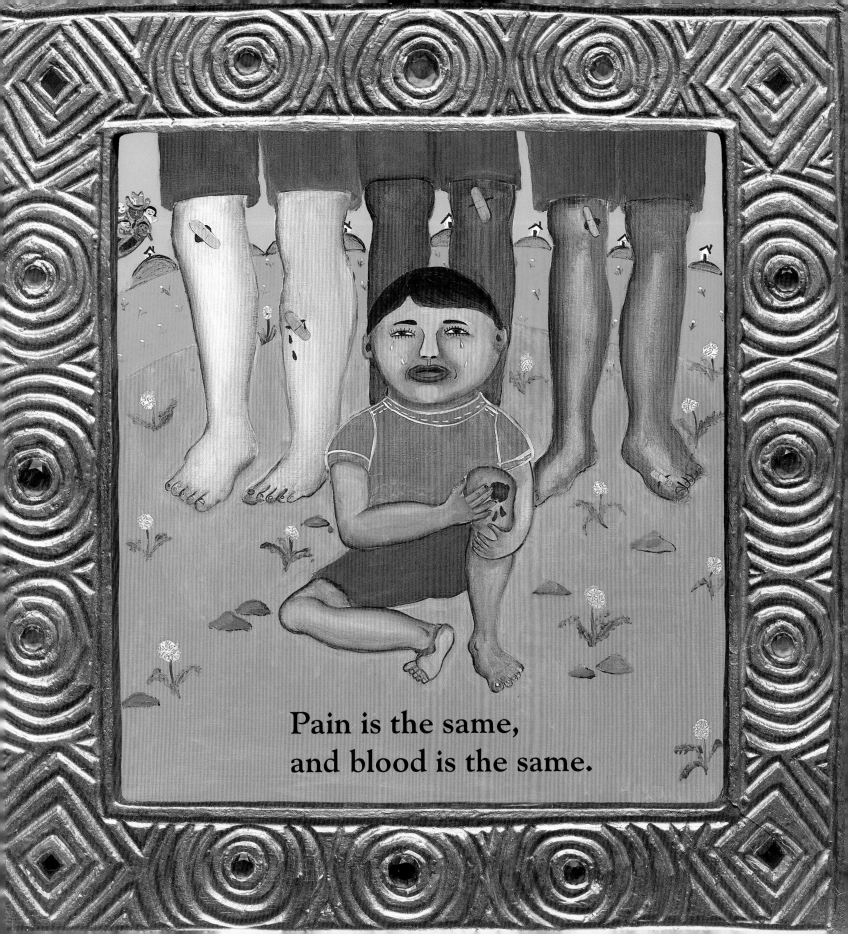

Pain is the same,
and blood is the same.

Smiles are the same,
and hearts are just the same—
wherever they are,
wherever you are,
wherever we are,

all over the world.